The Pips

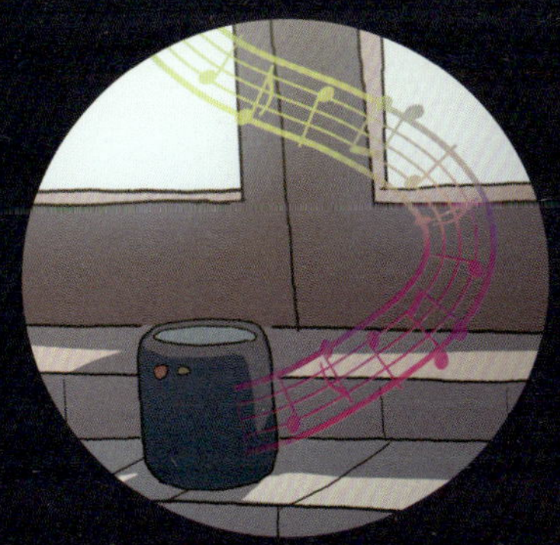

Written by
Daisy Hawkins

Illustrated by
Amerigo Pinelli

Zan is the tops.
Will Zan get a job?
I will go
to the top.
I will be the
fans' pick.

Zan gets a job.
It is not jazz – it is pop.

It is **Zan and The Pips**.

We will go to the top. We will be the fans' pick.

Ross is in The Pips, but
Ross is bad. Ross yells a lot.

Ross yells at Zan.
Ross yells at The Pips.

Zan is fed up. Will Zan quit?

Yes. Zan quits.

Bob is at the gig.
Bob tells The Pips Ross is bad.
Ross can go. I will fix it.

But Zan is the tops. I am into **Zan and The Pips.**

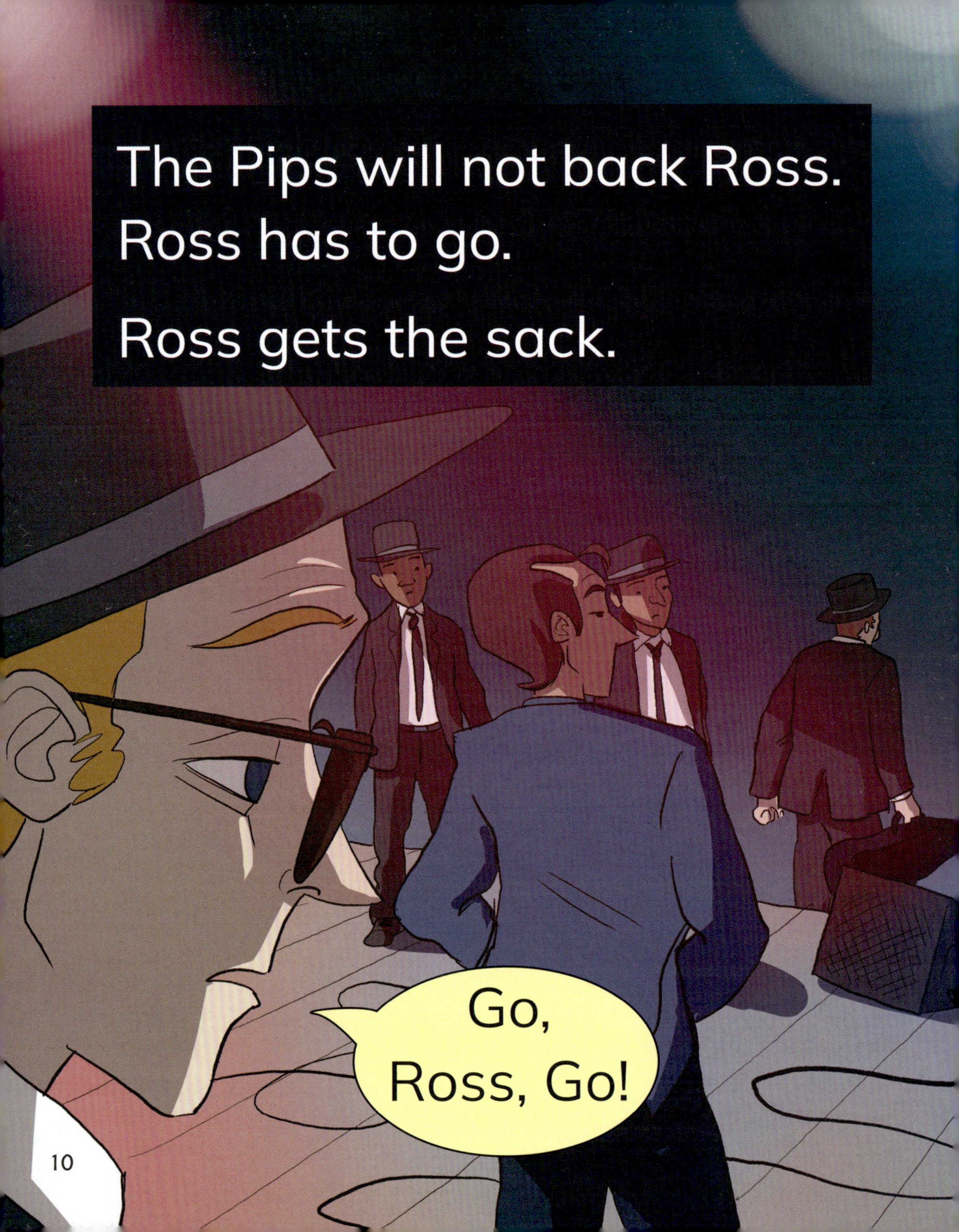

The Pips will not back Ross.
Ross has to go.

Ross gets the sack.

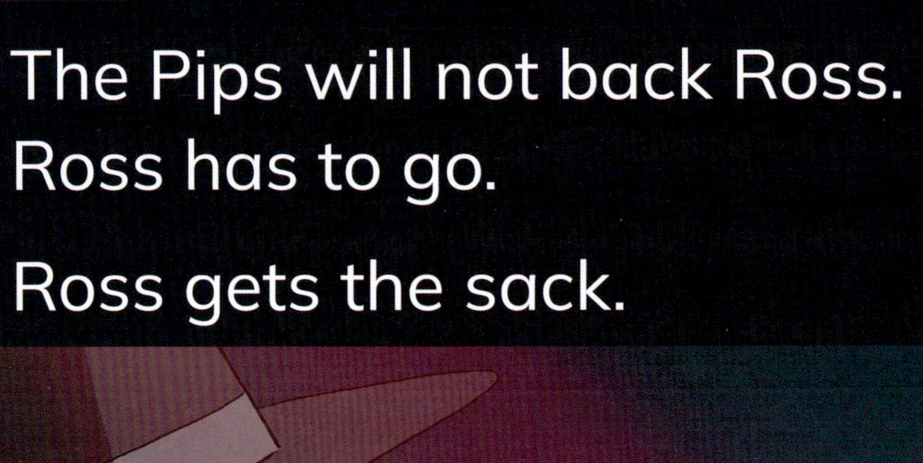

Zan did not quit.

Zan picks The Pips.

Bob gets Zan and The Pips into the top ten.
It is a quick pop hit.
The Pips
The Pips